THE CUPCAKE BANDIT

by Linda Van Regenmorter

Layout and design: Lauren Driscoll
Illustrator: Susan Lavalley Weaver
Publishing Consultant: Steven Adler WoW! Publishing and Distribution
Printed in the United States of America

Dedication

To my grandchildren
who are a continual source of inspiration and delight:

Karly, Alina, Bryce, Annabelle, Alexa & Hope

"They're gone! What happened?"
Grandma cried.

The cupcakes that Grandma and
Annabelle made had sat on the kitchen
table on a special dish with a top layer
and bottom layer.

Grandma had arrived a couple of days before for a visit while Annabelle's daddy was away on a trip for his job.

Yesterday had been special because Annabelle stayed home from preschool. While big sister Alina was at school and little sister Alexa was away at daycare, she and Grandma made cupcakes together. Not just any cupcakes. Rainbow cupcakes!

Their big dog Trooper watched every move as Grandma read the directions on the cake mix box and poured everything into a big bowl. While Grandma ran the mixer, Annabelle placed a paper cupcake holder in each section of the muffin pan.

Soon Annabelle was scooping a big spoonful of cake batter into each cupcake holder. "Yum!" Annabelle said as she licked the beaters.

Into the oven the cupcakes went. Grandma set the timer, and Trooper and Annabelle watched through the oven door. When the timer buzzed, Annabelle jumped up and down. "Grandma, they're done!"

Grandma said, "But the frosting has to wait until the cupcakes are cool." While they waited, Grandma read to Annabelle her favorite storybook about a dog who always got into trouble. Trooper played with his rubber bone toy and enjoyed the story too.

Grandma finally announced, "Now they've cooled off!" Annabelle clapped her hands. The fun part began! Grandma and Annabelle sat at the kitchen table and spread blue frosting on each one. Then Annabelle placed the rainbow candy on top and little marshmallows to look like clouds.

Sometimes she reached under the table
and gave some candy to Trooper who
loved sweets and quickly gobbled it up.
Annabelle grinned. "These are the cutest
cupcakes I've ever seen!" She decorated
a special cupcake for her daddy to have
when he came home.

When Mommy, Alina, and Alexa came home that afternoon, Annabelle and Trooper rushed outside to meet them. "Come see my pretty rainbow cupcakes!" Annabelle said.

All of them enjoyed one, and Mommy said they were the best cupcakes she had ever tasted. Mommy placed the cupcakes  in the middle of the kitchen table on a special dish with a top layer and a bottom layer. Annabelle was so proud! She could hardly wait to share her special cupcake with Daddy the next day when he got home from his trip.

11

That morning Grandma was the first to notice that there were only three cupcakes left on the special dish. They were at the very top of the dish, and the rest of the cupcakes were gone! What could have happened to all the cupcakes? There was a piece of rainbow candy on the floor and also a few crumbs, but nothing else was left of the missing cupcakes.

Everyone at breakfast was talking about what could have happened to the cupcakes. Had someone in the family gotten up during the night for a cupcake snack?

Had Mommy decided to put most of the cupcakes away in a safe place for later?

Where had all the cupcakes gone? Was it possible that someone had sneaked into their house during the night and eaten all those cupcakes? Could there be a cupcake bandit in the neighborhood?

Suddenly Alina noticed that Trooper was laying in his bed with a sad face. "Aw, what's wrong, Trooper? Aren't you feeling good?" Trooper raised his head and looked up at her, and it was then the three sisters noticed that Trooper had blue frosting fur on his chin!

Alexa opened her mouth into a big "Oh!" and Alina and Annabelle laughed and laughed. Trooper was the cupcake bandit! And now he was BUSTED and had a big tummy ache.

ABOUT THE AUTHOR

Linda Van Regenmorter grew up in Iowa and attended Northwestern College and the University of Minnesota. She worked as a self-employed medical transcriptionist and as a support to her husband Wayne as he served in various churches and with their church denomination in California, Minnesota, Iowa, South Dakota, Indiana, and Florida. Now they are enjoying their retirement in Parrish, Florida, which has allowed Linda to pursue her love of writing. Her other interests include reading, music, traveling, and animals. But Linda's greatest joy has always been family, and she considers them to be the most treasured blessings in her life.

ACKNOWLEDGEMENTS

First of all, a heartfelt thank you to my husband Wayne who has been my biggest supporter and cheerleader, encouraging me to pursue my dream. To the very talented team who made this book possible, I cannot thank you enough: Steve Adler of Wow! Publishing and Promotions for all the expert and excellent guidance every step of the way; Susan Lavalley Weaver, illustrator extraordinaire, whose quality work is second to none; and Lauren Driscoll, graphic designer, who so magically put all the pieces together. A special thanks goes to Ronni Miller who helped lay the foundation for this story and was invaluable in all the fine tuning along the way. Above all, may the glory go to God. It is my sincere hope that His joy and blessing will be found by all who read this book. May it rekindle the love of family and add some laughter to your day.

CPSIA information can be obtained
at www.ICGtesting.com
Printed in the USA
LVHW010248091121
702685LV00002B/18